THE MOUND BUILDERS

By the same author

THE CAVE HUNTERS

ANCIENT ELEPHANTS

PREHISTORIC MAN AND THE PRIMATES

THE FIRST MAMMALS

PREHISTORIC ANIMALS

The
Mound Builders

Written and illustrated by

WILLIAM E. SCHEELE

Director, Cleveland Museum of Natural History

THE WORLD PUBLISHING COMPANY

CLEVELAND AND NEW YORK

The author wishes to thank Olaf H. Prufer, anthropologist at the Cleveland Museum of Natural History, for his critical reading of the manuscript.

Published by The World Publishing Company

2231 West 110th Street, Cleveland 2, Ohio

Published simultaneously in Canada by

Nelson, Foster & Scott Ltd.

Library of Congress Catalog Card Number: 60-11463

FIRST EDITION

THE MOUND BUILDERS

WHEN the first explorers and settlers in North America began pushing inland from the eastern and southern coasts of what is now the United States, they found many high cone-shaped mounds, or strange low ridges of earth overgrown with trees or brambles that were clearly not natural forms. They had been made by man. But who were the men, and where were they?

In the South, the Spanish explorers soon met Indians who built mounds. These people were the Natchez and other related tribes, whose rich dress, strange ceremonies, temples, and slaves were strikingly different from other Indians living there at that time. The spectacular flat-topped mounds made by these people show a considerable influence from the great Indian cultures of Mexico and Central America.

A temple mound of the Southeastern Indians

But elsewhere in the East and Midwest, most of the man-made humps and ridges had been abandoned long ago. The ground near-by was often strewn with arrow points, pieces of pottery, bones, and many other signs of Indian activity, but no one—not

[8]

even the Indians living in that region—knew who the mound builders were.

Thousands of these Indian mounds were found, ranging from Florida to lower Canada, and from the Atlantic coast to the Mississippi and Missouri River valleys. And whenever people began to settle in a new territory, they found "Indian relics," an expression that came to mean any Indian object—from arrowheads, axheads, and beads to skeletons and mounds.

Normal, human curiosity about the mounds prompted people to dig into them. The exciting things they found remain a challenge to puzzle over and study even today. From these rich finds, a legend developed about the mysterious habits and origins of mound-building Indians.

Who were the Mound Builders? To answer correctly is difficult, for there is no single, simple answer. Most of the Indians who built mounds of earth were prehistoric peoples

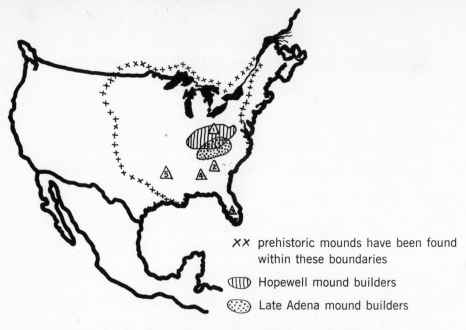

XX prehistoric mounds have been found within these boundaries

(|||) Hopewell mound builders

(∷∷) Late Adena mound builders

Important mound-builder sites
1. Hopewell (Ohio)   2. Etowah (Georgia)
3. Key Marco (Florida)   4. Moundville (Alabama)
5. Spiro (Oklahoma)
(not all sites date from the same period)

who disappeared from the face of the land before Columbus reached the outer islands of the North American continent.

The great Stone Age society of prehistoric Indians who lived in the Ohio River valley —people who had been dead for centuries when the first white men arrived in North

America—were Mound Builders. So were the Indians whom early Spanish explorers found in the South. Yet these two different kinds of Indians lived many hundreds of years apart. Nor was this practice true only of Indians. Many other primitive people all over the world were Mound Builders too.

No one is certain when or where the practice of mound-building began, or when it ended. In North America, Indians were constructing earth-mounds three thousand years ago, from before the time of Christ until well after De Soto explored the Mississippi River valley in 1541 A.D.

The name "Mound Builders" can apply to many different types of primitive peoples

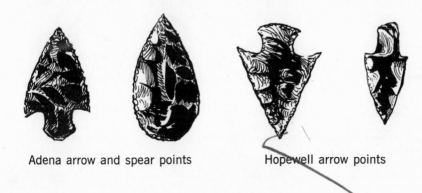

Adena arrow and spear points   Hopewell arrow points

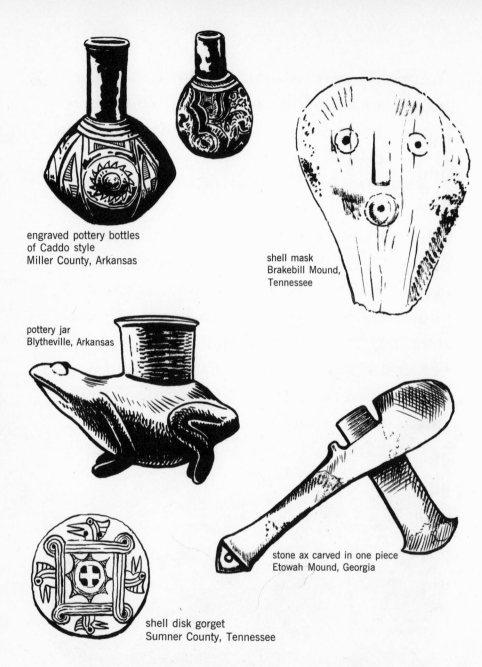

engraved pottery bottles
of Caddo style
Miller County, Arkansas

shell mask
Brakebill Mound,
Tennessee

pottery jar
Blytheville, Arkansas

stone ax carved in one piece
Etowah Mound, Georgia

shell disk gorget
Sumner County, Tennessee

*Objects found in Southern mounds (not drawn to same
scale and not from same time period as Hopewell mounds)*

in North America and throughout the world, but to most archaeologists it has come to mean the prehistoric Indians of the Ohio River valley.

Just as mounds were built by many different Indians in North America, they were also built for many different purposes. Some Indian mounds were built to be burial places, but others were merely symbolic shapes and contained nothing. Many mounds found in the South were once the foundations of wooden temples. Most mounds stand alone in the wilderness, offering no clue to their use or to the identity of their makers.

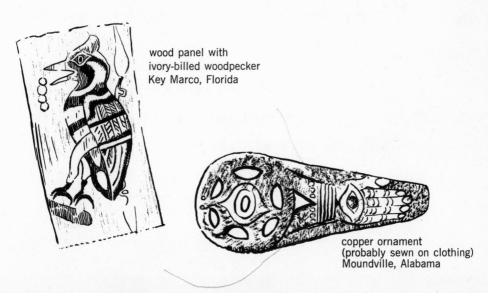

wood panel with
ivory-billed woodpecker
Key Marco, Florida

copper ornament
(probably sewn on clothing)
Moundville, Alabama

Partly because Indian mounds were so widespread, and partly because they had never seen living Mound Builders, American colonists had a great curiosity about them. Important scholarly societies and clubs were formed to study Indians, and many early books printed in the United States were about them. Some authors attempted to reconstruct the details of prehistoric Indian life and to describe the tools, weapons, and ornaments which had been found. Among the thousands of objects discovered, those picked up near mounds were especially interesting.

During the first 350 years of this country's growth, however, there was little interest in opening a mound to make a scientific study, or in sorting and caring for the specimens taken from mounds and village sites. The best discoveries were kept as curiosities; imperfect fragments were tossed aside. As recently as the 1930's, broken pieces of artifacts,

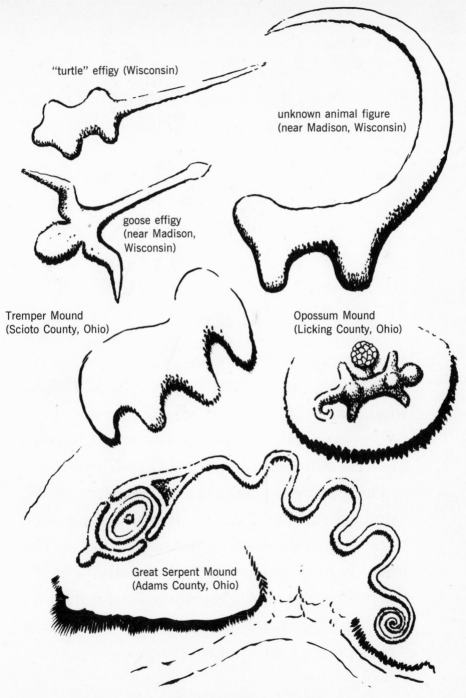

"turtle" effigy (Wisconsin)

unknown animal figure
(near Madison, Wisconsin)

goose effigy
(near Madison,
Wisconsin)

Tremper Mound
(Scioto County, Ohio)

Opossum Mound
(Licking County, Ohio)

Great Serpent Mound
(Adams County, Ohio)

Some mounds were shaped to resemble animals

The Wooden Deer Mask, found underwater at Key Marco,
Florida, is considered the best of all mound-builder masks

flint flakes, and faulty specimens of Indian
workmanship were usually discarded. Col-
lectors and even some early museums kept
only perfect specimens.

Diggers very often found great treasures,
but in a rush to get at unusual ornaments,
they overlooked valuable clues that might
have helped to explain the daily lives of
those who had built mounds. As archaeologists learned more about their own science,

they slowed down their digging crews and looked more sharply for details in the earth.

Today, careful diagrams are drawn at every stage of digging. Faint traces of color or a change in the earth's composition are carefully studied for clues to perishable materials which are seldom or never preserved. Scientists studying an Indian site include for comparison every scrap of evidence; flint flakes and broken pieces of finished work are as important to the record as are the rarer perfect specimens.

New methods of settling questions about the age of discoveries have also been established in the laboratory. Before World War II, the

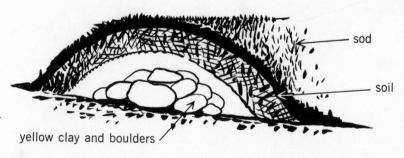

sod

soil

yellow clay and boulders

Cross section of the Great Serpent Mound. Although it contains no Indian bones or artifacts, it is 1,254 feet long and from three to five feet in height

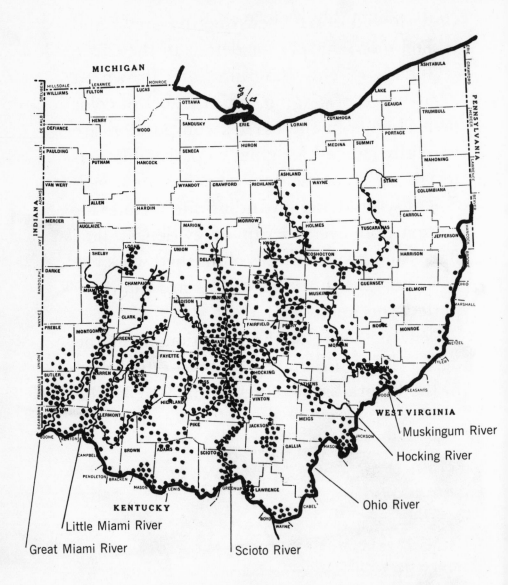

Mound-builder earthworks in southern Ohio

only reasonably accurate information for the dates of prehistoric North American Indian remains, came from the Southwestern states. There, the climate and the protected position of many deposits made it possible to find undisturbed soil, bones, and other specimens. The tree rings in timbers which had been used in Indian pueblos could be compared to growth rings from living trees. This method of dating made it possible to trace the age of Indian sites in the Southwest as far back as 11 A.D., but it is no help at all in dating Eastern archaeological sites.

Even tree-ring data were lacking in the Midwestern and Eastern United States, where weather, erosion, years of farming, and vigorous collecting of relics ruined any chance of dating a discovery. The great amount of material found in the Eastern states was also confusing, since recent Indians had lived and died on village sites that previously had been lived upon by many different tribes for centuries.

Since 1945, three important means of estimating the age of prehistoric materials have been perfected. Analysis of ancient plant-pollen grains, and measurement of fluorine content in bones or similar porous materials, help modern scholars to sort and establish the age of prehistoric finds. The most reliable tool used so far in studying the remains of Mound Builders, however, is the system of dating by measuring the amount of Carbon 14, or radiocarbon, found in certain substances. Bones, wood, shell, bark,

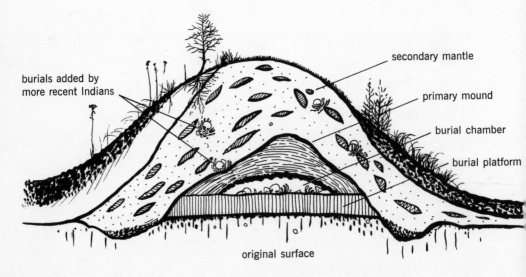

secondary mantle

burials added by
more recent Indians

primary mound

burial chamber

burial platform

original surface

Cross section of a typical burial mound

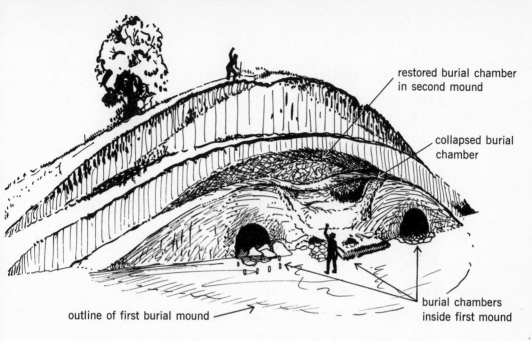

restored burial chamber
in second mound

collapsed burial
chamber

burial chambers
inside first mound

outline of first burial mound

How a mound is excavated. This is the Seip Mound

corncobs, seeds, and many other materials from archaeological diggings can now be checked to learn their age.

From the vast number of primitive Indian treasures that have been collected, and in spite of inevitable confusion during the early years of the young science of archaeology, some conclusions about Mound Builders have now been reached. One important fact established by archaeologists is that building mounds was by no means the most remarkable achievement of these Indians.

The Indians who best fit our concept of "Mound Builders" have long been extinct. They were unique because even for centuries before Christ they were no longer wandering hunters. They were farmers who lived in one place the year round, harvested crops, and stored them for winter use. They were artists and traders, too, whose expeditions journeyed throughout most of North America. And their religious beliefs were well developed, with very complex burial rites.

The most interesting of these Indians lived in the valleys of the Ohio River and its tributary streams. They are known as the Hopewell Indians, a name derived from a site of thirty-eight mounds located in Ross County, Ohio, on lands once owned by Captain M. C. Hopewell.

The landscape of prehistoric Ohio was by

A Hopewell village (artist's conception based on pattern of an Adena excavation). The structure at left is a platform burial

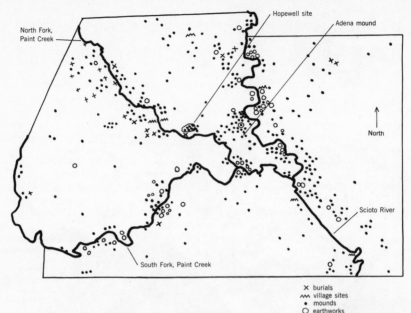

Mound-builder sites in Ross County, Ohio

no means entirely suited to Indian villages and farms. The northwest corner of the state was wet, much of it covered by vast swamps. The heavily wooded northeast was a tangle of bogs, ponds, and dense woods. The southeast corner consisted of narrow valleys and steep, rocky hills. The remaining one third of the state, including Ross County, was rolling and more open, bounded to the south

[24]

by the broad, beautiful Ohio River—a land ideally suited to the needs of a farming people.

Indian mounds are not always easy to recognize, though some of the largest are at least 100 feet high and cover many acres. Such large mounds are not common; where they exist they are important landmarks. Some mounds were the result of building one mound on top of another until as many as a dozen were contained in the same hill of earth.

Cone-shaped Hopewell mounds are often grouped together. Low earth ridges built in geometric patterns of circles, squares, or other

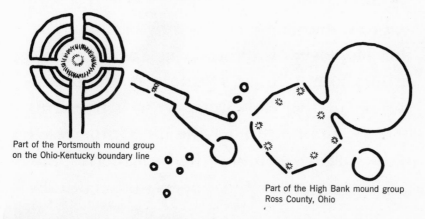

Part of the Portsmouth mound group
on the Ohio-Kentucky boundary line

Part of the High Bank mound group
Ross County, Ohio

Earthworks in geometric patterns around mounds are distinctive of Hopewell mound builders

simple shapes are included with them or connect them. Shallow ditches near the earthworks show where the soil was removed to make the mound.

In those places where fields are farmed to the very base of mounds, the work of the Indians stands out clearly, but just as often trees and brush cover and hide the lower mounds. In many of the Midwestern states, important sites are being found today in landscapes that were once overlooked as likely digging places. Small mounds often prove to be as full of material as the largest. Size is no measure of a mound's importance or use.

From radiocarbon dating we know that the Hopewell Indians built their mounds from about 400 B.C. to 400 A.D. Adena ancestors to the Hopewells were active from 850 B.C. until well after the more progressive Hopewell tribes had settled southern Ohio.

The Hopewells have been unsuccessfully

This Hopewell pot fragment (left) is engraved and cord marked; the Adena fragment (right) is plain

compared to the people who built the flat-topped earth-mounds found in the south-eastern United States. Art that helps to identify each of the two peoples may be similar, but no proof of contact between them is possible.

No one knows the origin of the Hopewell Indians or how their culture developed, but perhaps the most important comparison among Hopewell and other prehistoric peoples is made in their burial practices. Like many peoples in northern Asia and along the northwest coast of North America, the Hopewells constructed log tombs, made platform burials and re-burials, and painted bones of

[27]

the dead with ochre. This does not mean that there was a real connection among these peoples, but there is a hint that the Hopewellian Mound Builders kept many traits of their Asiatic origin.

The land occupied by Hopewell people and their Adena ancestors included a vast territory, at least ten present-day states. Hopewell villages and trading outposts reached from the Gulf of Mexico to Wisconsin, and from New York and Pennsylvania to Missouri. The heart of this empire was the Ohio River valley, with the principal Hopewell mound groups near a smaller river now known as the Scioto.

Nothing archaeologists have learned about these Indians from their tools, weapons, ornaments, or houses and mound patterns shows any sign that outside influences—either ideas or an invasion by force—suddenly affected Hopewell customs. The Hopewell mound-building culture seems to have developed

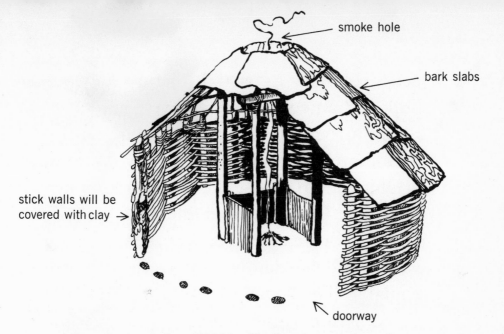

smoke hole

bark slabs

stick walls will be
covered with clay →

← doorway

*Adena house (after Webb). Similar houses must have
been used by Hopewell people*

gradually in the same river valleys that their
ancestors had lived in for many centuries.

Like ancient Egyptian nobles, important
Hopewell leaders were buried in splendor.
The ordinary tribesman who farmed, hunted,
and labored to build mounds and temples
and the outstanding craftsman both knew
that their best work was destined to be buried
when one of their tribal leaders died. Because
of this practice, modern archaeologists can

piece together a partial picture of what Hopewellian culture must have been.

About the time Christ was born, a group of Hopewell chiefs in what is now the State of Ohio met to choose the location for a new burial site. Close by was a fine place for a village, a spot near a river where fish, game, water, and gardening soil were all easily available. The boundaries they staked for the sacred area enclosed about 130 acres which were part of a flat terrace two hundred yards from the river (now called Paint Creek). To the east and west were smaller streams; to the north was the gullied edge of a higher terrace from which several springs flowed. Both terraces were lightly overgrown with brush and trees which could be easily cleared.

Near-by, in stream beds and soil banks, was a good supply of clay, sand, gravel, and flat stones. These were within easy carrying distance of future mounds.

The powerful priest group who guided the

Hopewell and Adena people raised corn, but they also ate everything else the land provided

tribe was well pleased with the choice of land. The view from the future temples would be impressive, for many rugged tree-covered hills were in sight. Only four miles away was the ancient Adena mound; a mile beyond it lay the Scioto River valley. Adena people were the honored ancestors of the Hopewell tribes; the dead of both peoples had been buried in or near this valley for centuries. In fact, there was no clear-cut division be-

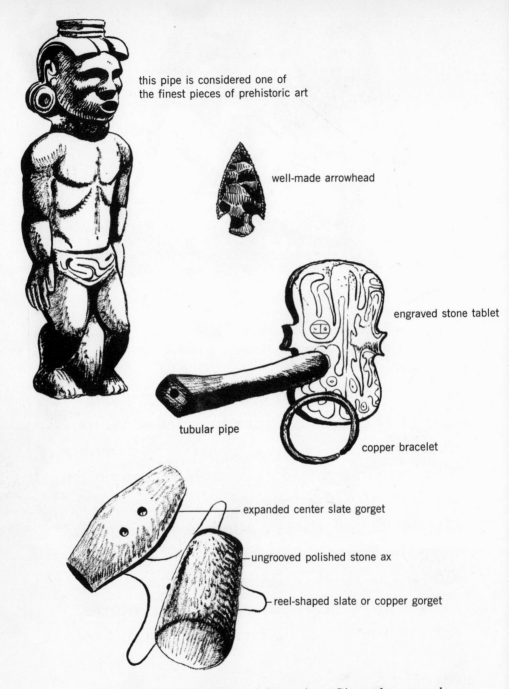

this pipe is considered one of
the finest pieces of prehistoric art

well-made arrowhead

engraved stone tablet

tubular pipe

copper bracelet

expanded center slate gorget

ungrooved polished stone ax

reel-shaped slate or copper gorget

Typical objects found in Adena sites. Since these people were ancestors of the Hopewells, the two styles of work are mixed in some sites

flint or obsidian blades
and points in
eccentric shapes

dippers and containers
made from
marine conch shells

chunks
of ochre

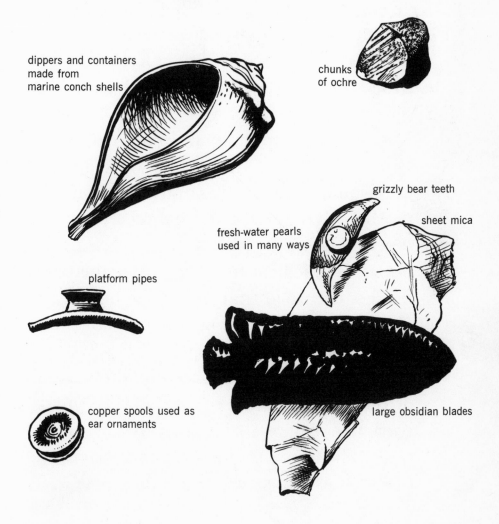

grizzly bear teeth

sheet mica

fresh-water pearls
used in many ways

platform pipes

copper spools used as
ear ornaments

large obsidian blades

These objects are distinctive of the Hopewell culture

tween the Adena and Hopewell Indians. Living relatives of both peoples occupied every stream valley within easy traveling distance from this new village location.

The chief, the tribal priests, the great hunters, and the expedition leaders of the tribe were all deeply concerned about the ceremonial site they were about to build. Their tribe was prominent in a great Indian nation, and they themselves were men of importance. Their artists and craftsmen were the best living; even the baskets, pots, and weaving done by the women were exceptional. It is logical to assume that the tribal leaders dreamed that this place near Paint Creek would someday be known as the finest achievement of their people.

Once the decision concerning the location of the future mound area had been made, workmen began to clear away brush and trees. The thud of stone axes and the crackle of fires must have been heard for weeks while sweating laborers went about their tasks. The best timber and some saplings were saved for future building; everything else was burned. A low rectangular ridge of earth was required to mark off the ceremonial compound. This was quickly under construction. A smaller square area and a circle were added to the pattern of ridges. These ridges were typical of Hopewell sites; they marked the boundaries of ceremonial activity. Openings were left in the ridges for the entrance of processions.

Hundreds of workers laboriously carried baskets and skin-aprons full of earth to places under construction. Diggers used sticks, clam-shell hoes, and shoulder blades of large game animals to loosen the soil that was needed. It took a long time to finish this job. The Hope-wellians had no work animals and, of course, no earth-moving machinery to help push piles of loose dirt into position.

While work on the sacred enclosure continued, bark-covered houses were being built

Building a burial mound. Earth was carried to the mound in slings, pouches, and baskets of bark and twigs

in the village. Generally five or six houses were clustered together, sometimes according to the kind of work done by the inhabitants. Gardens were planted in well-watered soil near the creek, and corn, beans, squash, and tobacco flourished. Roots, nuts, and berries were gathered in the wild places near the village. Storage pits, lined with rocks and clay, were dug between the homes. Corn and other durable foods were kept in these for winter use.

The work of settling in a new place must

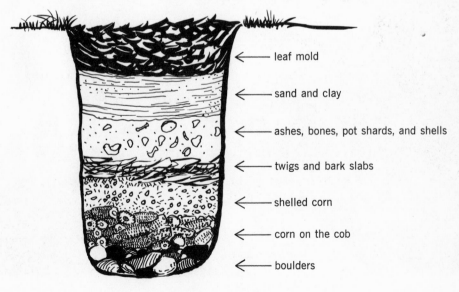

←——— leaf mold

←——— sand and clay

←——— ashes, bones, pot shards, and shells

←——— twigs and bark slabs

←——— shelled corn

←——— corn on the cob

←——— boulders

A food storage pit

have gone on for months. While it continued, expeditions set out for distant places to secure exotic raw materials for tribal artisans. Men traveled to the Rocky Mountains to get obsidian, a hard volcanic rock, and grizzly-bear teeth. Other groups went as far as the Gulf of Mexico for shark teeth, conch shells, and sea-turtle shells. Copper pits in Michigan, Wisconsin, and Minnesota were the source of chunks and nuggets of copper, which was used on many things distinctive of Hopewell work.

These trading trips of the Hopewell Indians were one of the truly remarkable things about them. They knew a great deal about the North American continent and developed a network of trading contacts with other Indians. Because of such trips, their tribe was well organized and strengthened by a knowledge of the habits and weaknesses of their rivals.

Powerful medicine men, or priests, gave

direction and meaning to the lives of the working Indians and their leaders. Religious beliefs were centered around the rites honoring dead tribal leaders. Accordingly, much of the work done in the village was in preparation for burial ceremonies.

Long before the first burial took place, workers cleared away loose soil from a spot within the sacred enclosure. They spread

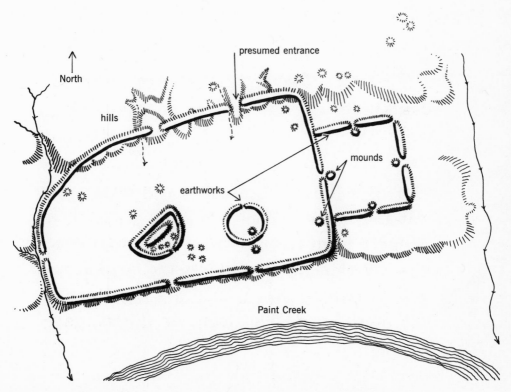

Plan of the Hopewell mound group, Ross County, Ohio

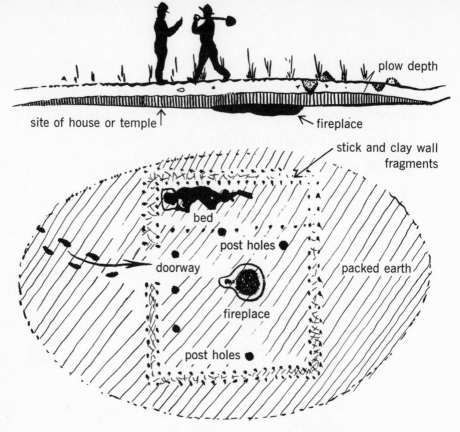

Floor plan of a Hopewell house or temple

clay over the exposed earth and tramped it
flat and smooth. Then sand and gravel were
brought from the river and spread over the
clay. Workmen followed quickly to set poles,
which marked the outline of a temple, into
the damp clay. The walls of the building

[40]

were woven of branches and twigs and plastered with a layer of chopped twigs and clay. The roof poles were covered with slabs of tree bark as protection against the weather. With the completion of a temple, the spiritual beliefs of the tribe could be served.

This building also played a vital part in the villagers' daily lives. The largest temple room was a meeting place where the important men came to listen to their chief and the priests. A smaller room contained a clay fire-basin surrounded by rare carvings and pots. The center of a second small room featured a tomb made of logs and stones.

In this building, screened from the stares of children and the common working people, the men of the tribe met to retell their legends and share their wisdom with a younger generation destined to be priests or leaders. Like all people of the Hopewell community, those who came to the sacred building respected and feared the authority of the few among them whose rank permitted them to wear copper helmets and shirts that glistened with ornaments of mica, silver, and pearls. At meeting times pipes were smoked and reed flutes, bound with silver and copper, were played softly in the dim smoky interior.

Hopewell clothing was simple, for the climate was mild most of the time. Men wore breechcloths; women used wrap-around

The hair style of this flute player was taken from a clay figure. The flute is bound in copper

Hopewell men in their best clothing. Pearls, copper, animals' claws, teeth, and jawbones were used as ornaments; the swastika is a common mound-builder figure

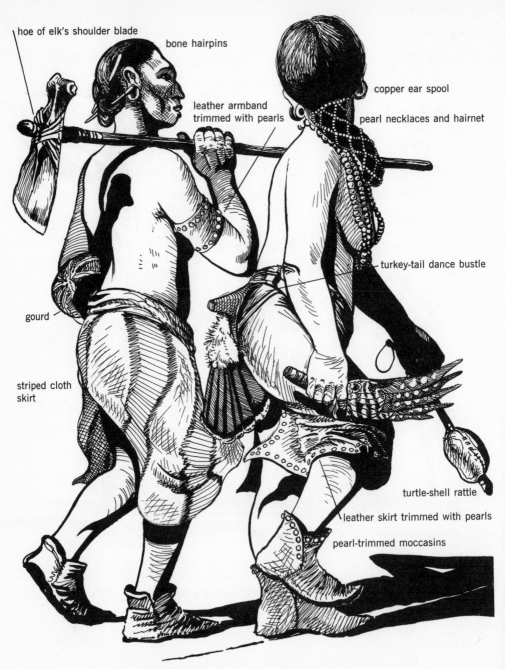

hoe of elk's shoulder blade

bone hairpins

leather armband
trimmed with pearls

copper ear spool

pearl necklaces and hairnet

turkey-tail dance bustle

gourd

striped cloth
skirt

turtle-shell rattle

leather skirt trimmed with pearls

pearl-trimmed moccasins

*Two Hopewell women, a dancer and a gardener
(drawing based on clay figures)*

skirts. Such clothing was decorated with painted stripes and looping curved lines, pearls, and flat ornaments. Decorated leather, fur, or cloth shirts and capes were worn during ceremonials. Sandals, leggings, and bootlike moccasins were also worn. Hair styles were intricate, and for special occasions faces and bodies were painted.

Mica, copper, and pearls were plentiful. Some people used these materials as exchange for valuable goods. Pearls, in particular, were used in the same way as later Indians used shell wampum.

Not long after the Paint Creek village was completed and the people had settled into a normal routine of daily life, the priests decided to make an offering to their dead leaders. This was to be a rare display of power, so hundreds of valued possessions were gathered together. These included plain and fancy pipes, as well as ornaments of varied materials—slate, quartz, mica, copper, iron, flint, bone, silver, and shell—and many unusual stone objects. There were also pieces of treasured galena, hematite, and pyrite that had not been worked. The finest piece of the entire offering was a replica of a human head made of pounded copper. At the priests' orders this store of wealth was covered by a mound within the temple.

After such an impressive beginning, it seemed certain that the Paint Creek village would win an important place in Hopewell history, for few villages could afford to make such a gift. And for months after this mem-

The Hopewell pot at left was for burial use only; that at right was for daily use

A cremation ceremony inside a Hopewell temple (poses and ornaments are derived from clay figures found in the Turner group of mounds in Ohio)

A Hopewell craftsman at work (from a figure in the Ohio State Museum; each item is drawn from actual specimens)

orable event, the people of the village saw continuing proof of their tribe's greatness.

Every week, long columns of travel-weary slaves entered the settlement with loads of raw materials for the sculptors and other craftsmen. Painters added symbols, stripes, and curved shapes to long panels of cloth in tan, red, and black. Hundreds of lumpy fresh-water pearls were cleaned, drilled, and sewn on clothing or glued to ceremonial weapons. No one in the village was idle. The plans for the ceremonial rites were well organized, and everyone had his special job. All intended to please their leaders.

Within a few years of settling in this new place, the village workers were called upon to build several small burial mounds. The first burials must have been long-remembered because of the pearl necklace worn by the warrior whose body occupied the main grave. This string, containing 332 pearls, is the finest Hopewellian necklace ever discovered. A heavy cloth robe and large copper

Engraved human leg bone, typical of Hopewell mounds and unique to them. Copper head from Spiro, Oklahoma, showing hair style, headdress, and other ornaments

breastplate were also part of his burial costume. Some tools were placed in the grave, but the most distinctive addition was the dead warrior's trophy skull, that of an enemy chief he had killed many years before.

The bodies of two captive slaves, which were not decorated in any fashion, were also placed in this grave. All three were covered with a thick layer of tree bark, which helped preserve the buried splendor of this grave for nearly two thousand years, until modern archaeologists opened the mound at the beginning of this century.

As years passed, hundreds of burials of many kinds were added within the original sacred enclosure. The total number of skeletons found by archaeologists in the thirty-eight Hopewell mounds does not represent the entire population of the village that existed there, however. The common people of the tribe were apparently buried near their homes, or their bodies were burned or bundled and placed on platforms.

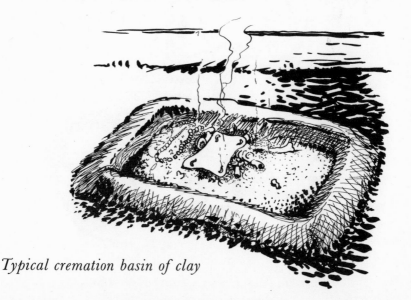

Typical cremation basin of clay

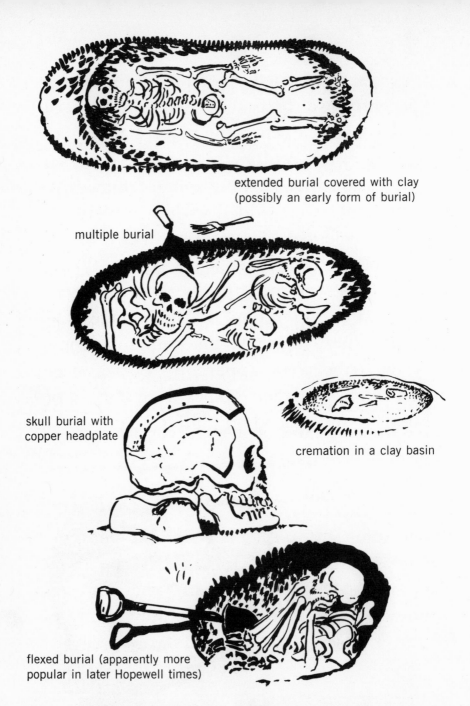

extended burial covered with clay
(possibly an early form of burial)

multiple burial

skull burial with
copper headplate

cremation in a clay basin

flexed burial (apparently more
popular in later Hopewell times)

Five kinds of Hopewell and Adena burials

Many undecorated skeletons were placed in burials along with elaborately ornamented bodies. From this we may assume that relatives or slaves were buried with Hopewell people of high rank, just as some early Egyptian burial chambers contain the families and servants of kings.

One such burial was that of a young noble and his wife. The couple were laid side by side in garments that glittered with pearls and copper buttons. Many bracelets, spool-shaped ornaments for the ears, breastplates, and beads were placed on both bodies. The six-foot man and his young wife wore necklaces of grizzly-bear teeth; their heavy black hair was shaped carefully and pinned in place with long copper rods. Extra jewelry and some unusual tools were laid along the edges of the grave. To preserve the facial beauty of this young couple, their natural noses were replaced by gleaming noses of pure copper. This elegant burial was just

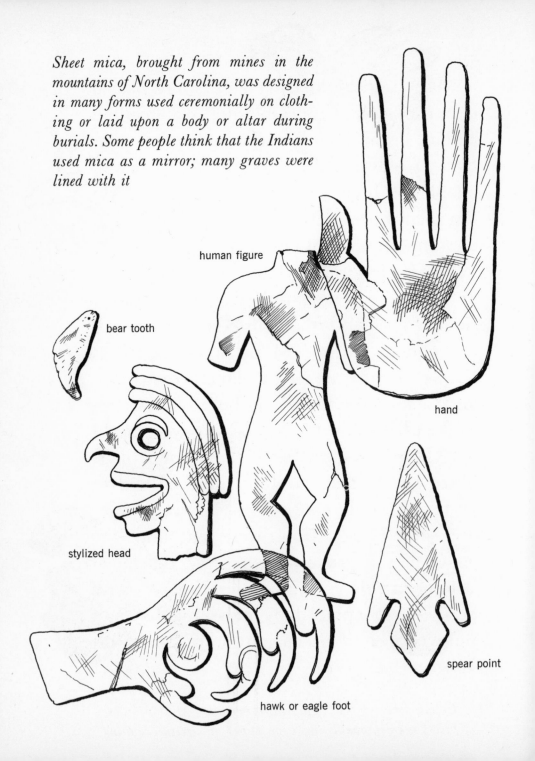

Sheet mica, brought from mines in the mountains of North Carolina, was designed in many forms used ceremonially on clothing or laid upon a body or altar during burials. Some people think that the Indians used mica as a mirror; many graves were lined with it

human figure

bear tooth

hand

stylized head

spear point

hawk or eagle foot

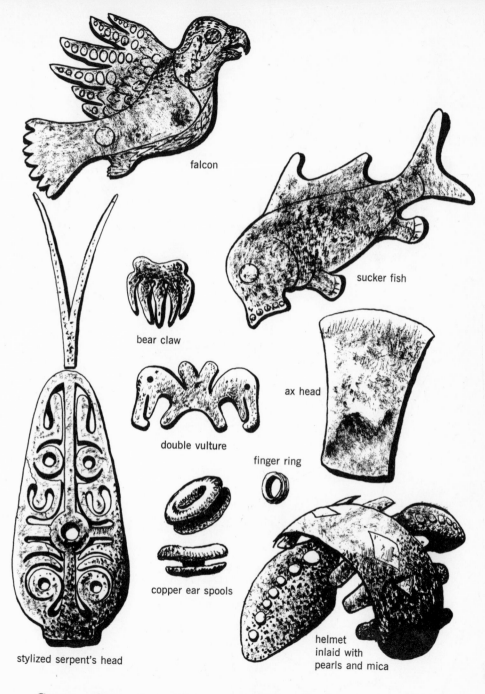

falcon

sucker fish

bear claw

double vulture

ax head

finger ring

copper ear spools

stylized serpent's head

helmet inlaid with pearls and mica

Copper objects from Hopewell mounds. Most of these pieces were probably sewn on capes or similar clothing

*Spectators line the earthworks to watch the building of a
log tomb. When it is finished, the tomb will be burned
and then covered*

one of the fifty included in one of the larger
mounds near this village.

By the time the Hopewell leaders decided
to abandon the Paint Creek village that had
been their home for many years, their people
had constructed many mounds of many
sizes. Within them, the tribal craftsmen left

an astounding record of their talents, proof that the Hopewell Indians were the most unusual prehistoric Indian group living in North America.

When Hopewellian Mound Builders began to move westward out of Ohio, most of their mound sites and enclosures remained silent and empty for about two hundred years. No one knows exactly why the Hopewells left, but perhaps the Eastern woodlands Indians were already invading the territory. We do know that, in time, these newcomers began to bury their dead in Hopewell mounds.

Hopewell designs on stone marbles found in the Seip Mound with the body of a young boy

falcon

wolf

human head
set with pearls

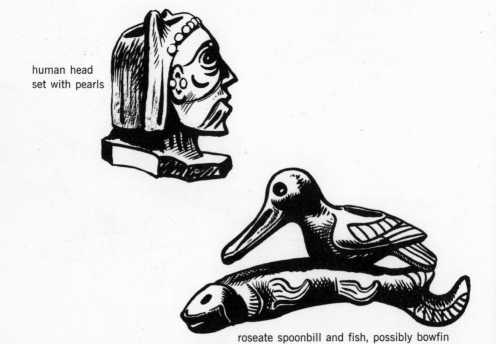

roseate spoonbill and fish, possibly bowfin

geese

toad

most typical form

vulture

Typical Hopewell platform effigy pipes (not drawn to same scale)

Hopewell hunters used spear throwers and bows

Hopewell Indians did not disappear suddenly, and there is evidence of their culture all over the central United States. But their well-organized ways and the fine quality of the things they made did diminish as they moved westward and south.

White explorers never saw Hopewell mounds when the Hopewell people were living near them and using them as the ceremonial settings they were intended to be. Other Indians built mounds before and after the Hopewells, but no Indians north of Mexico were ever more artistic. And nothing like the richness of their traditions was ever seen again among the Indians of North America.

ABOUT THE AUTHOR

WILLIAM E. SCHEELE, Director of the Cleveland Museum of Natural History, was born in Cleveland in 1920. He won scholarships in art and biology and was graduated from Western Reserve University in 1947. In November, 1939, he won the first annual Bird Art Contest sponsored by the Cleveland Museum of Natural History, and the next day he was a member of their staff. In 1949, after army service had interrupted his career, he was appointed director of the museum; he was then one of the youngest museum directors in the country. Mr. Scheele's outside activities include painting natural-history subjects (he has exhibited in many museums), fossil hunting, and school-board membership. He lives with his wife and three sons on a tree farm near Chardon, Ohio. He is the author of several books for young people, of which the most recent is *The Cave Hunters*.